D1272296

Just
Joking
DOGS

Get ready for
TAIL WAGGIN' FUN!

NATIONAL GEOGRAPHIC KiDS

Just Joking DOGS

Rosie Gowsell Pattison

NATIONAL GEOGRAPHIC
WASHINGTON, D.C.

Schnauzers were originally used to catch rats and other vermin. Their mustaches protected their faces from rat bites while hunting.
KNOCK,
KNOCK.
Who's there?
Interrupting Schnauzer.
Interrupting Schnau—
BARK BARK BARK BARK BARK!

Q What do you get if you cross a dog with a black-and-white ball?

A A soccer spaniel.

TONGUE TWISTER!

Say this fast three times:

The Rhodesian ridgeback ran round the rugged rock.

Q How do you stop a dog from barking in the back seat of a car?

A Put her in the front seat.

DOG 1: Did you see that black-and-white dog over there?

DOG 2: Wow! He looks like a bear!

DOG 1: Yes, isn't he panda-stic?

Dachshund means "badger dog" in German. These canines were originally bred for hunting badgers.

Poodles are the national dog of France. There, they are known as *caniche*, which means "duck dog."
KNOCK, KNOCK.
Who's there?
Poodles.
Poodles who?
It's raining so hard there are poodles everywhere.

Q

What is a dog's favorite breakfast?

A

Pooched eggs and barkon.

Q

Which dog will laugh at all of these jokes?

A

A Chi-ha-ha.

Q What's the biggest problem with corgi jokes?

A They're too short.

Q What did the dog bring on her camping trip?

A A pup-up tent.

Q How did the flea get from one dog to the other?

A It *itchhiked.*

Q Which dogs live in the Big Apple?

A New Yorkies.

Jackals are close canine cousins to dogs. They live in the savanna, bushlands, and deserts of west and central Africa.

TAIL
WAGGIN'
TALES

NAME: Ella Bean

BREED: Yorkshire terrier mix

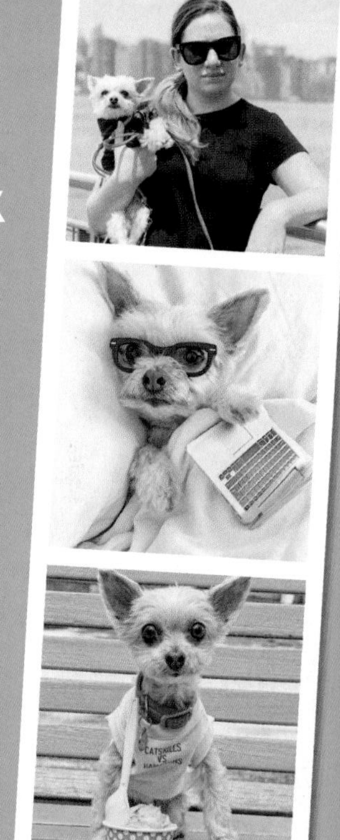

FIDO FACTS:

Ella Bean went from being a rescued pup to a globe-trotting, furry fashionista. This doggo diva has been photographed lounging on yachts, feasting on fancy dinners, and modeling the latest in Fido fashion all around the world. And while Ella Bean enjoys strutting her stuff on the ... *ahem* ... catwalk, her human is setting her sights on becoming a mongrel mogul with plans to launch her own clothing line for dogs. But Ella Bean doesn't forget her humble beginnings. She uses her popularity to raise awareness and money for pet rescues.

Ella Bean has two rescue dog sisters: Coconut and FiFi von Bean.

Ella Bean sleeps in a king-size bed.

She is also a foodie! Ella Bean feasts on fancy food, such as ceviche (a cold, raw fish dish), lobster, and salmon.

PLAYFUL PUPS

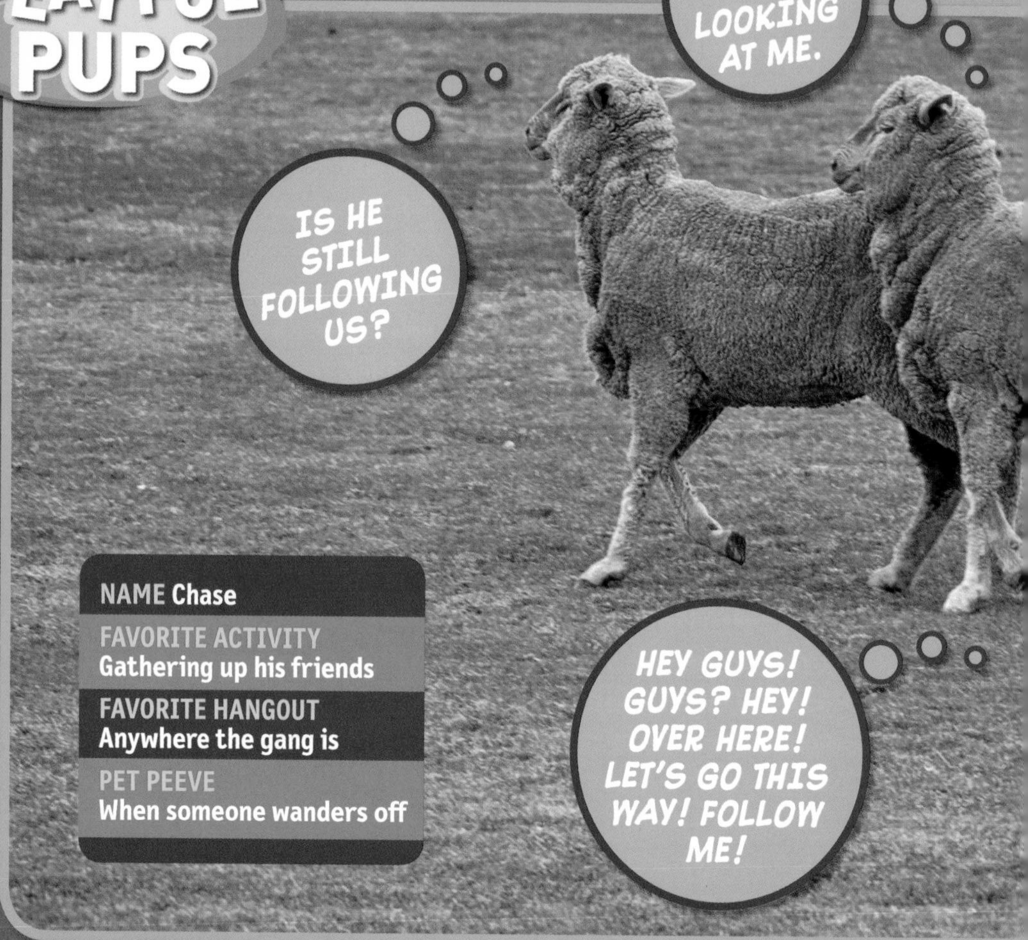

NAME Chase

FAVORITE ACTIVITY
Gathering up his friends

FAVORITE HANGOUT
Anywhere the gang is

PET PEEVE
When someone wanders off

MAYBE HE'S A WATCH DOG?

JOSÉ: Did you hear my dog ate all the Scrabble tiles?

LEANNE: Really? Is she OK?

JOSÉ: Yes, but she keeps leaving me little messages all over the yard.

Q **What do you get if you cross a wild dog and a breakfast food?**

A A flapjackal.

Bad Dog Handbook:
• TOILET BOWL: Source for water (see also: owner yelling)
• GARBAGE BAG: Source for food (see also: owner yelling)
• VACUUM CLEANER: Evildoer, avoid at all costs
• FIREWORKS: Sign that world is ending—mostly likely caused by the vacuum cleaner
• OWNER YELLING: Like barking, but for humans. Bark back, they seem to like it.

Q Where do dog scientists work?

A In *Lab*ratories.

Q Why did the mastiff wear pink fuzzy slippers?

A Because his green ones were in the wash.

Q What's the difference between a dog and a flea?

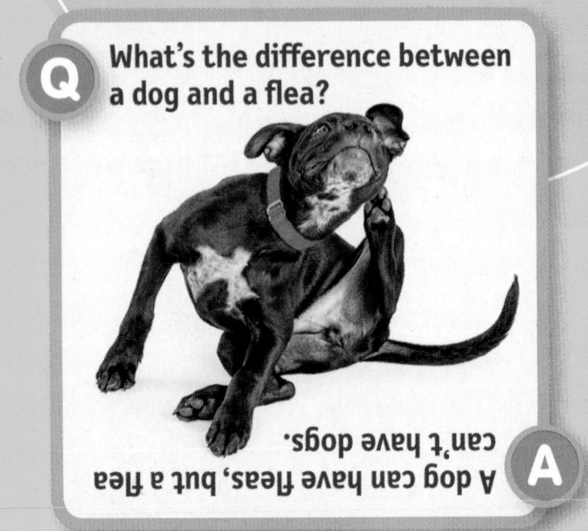

A A dog can have fleas, but a flea can't have dogs.

Q Why aren't dogs good dancers?

A Because they have two left feet.

A Jack Russell terrier can jump up to five feet (1.5 m) in the air.

Known for their distinctive howl, wolves are pack animals that often hunt prey together.
KNOCK,
KNOCK.
Who's there?
Wolf.
Wolf who?
Wolf you please open this door?
HA! HA! HA! HA! HA! HA! HA!

Q What kind of dog runs into a corner when it hears a bell?

A A boxer.

DOG OWNER: My dog's fur keeps falling out. What's happening?

VET: Let's see if I can shed some light on the problem.

KNOCK,
KNOCK.
Who's there?
Mutt.
Mutt who?
Mutt you always ask me that?

Dig, dig, dig. Terriers love to dig so much that it is a part of their name! "Terra" means "earth" in Latin. "Terroir" means "soil" in French.

TONGUE TWISTER!

Say this fast three times:

Pete the pinscher pinches people.

Q

What's black and white and red all over?

A Dalmatian with a sunburn.

A

Q

What do you get if you cross a foxhound and a giraffe?

A dog that can bark at airplanes.

A

Q

How did the dog feel about going to the dentist?

En-tooth-iastic!

A

DOGGONE FUNNY
I THINK MY NEW HAIRSTYLE IS QUITE FETCHING.

NAME: Luigi Maestro

BREED: Shih tzu

FIDO FACTS:

Most dogs love a car ride, but Luigi Maestro takes it to a whole new level! This classy canine owns a fleet of mutt-size luxury cars and can be found driving himself down the streets of New York City. OK, so even though Luigi's paws are on the wheel, it's actually his owner that drives the car with a remote control. But he still looks cool! A pooch-size Porsche, Fido-friendly Ferrari, and a barking Bentley are just a few of the cars in Luigi's collection. Make no bones about it, this is one lucky dog!

It's not just his garage that's impressive! Luigi's closet is full of posh driving outfits.

Luigi has appeared on a reality TV show in his black Mercedes-Benz.

He has more than 20,000 social media followers.

TAIL WAGGIN' TALES

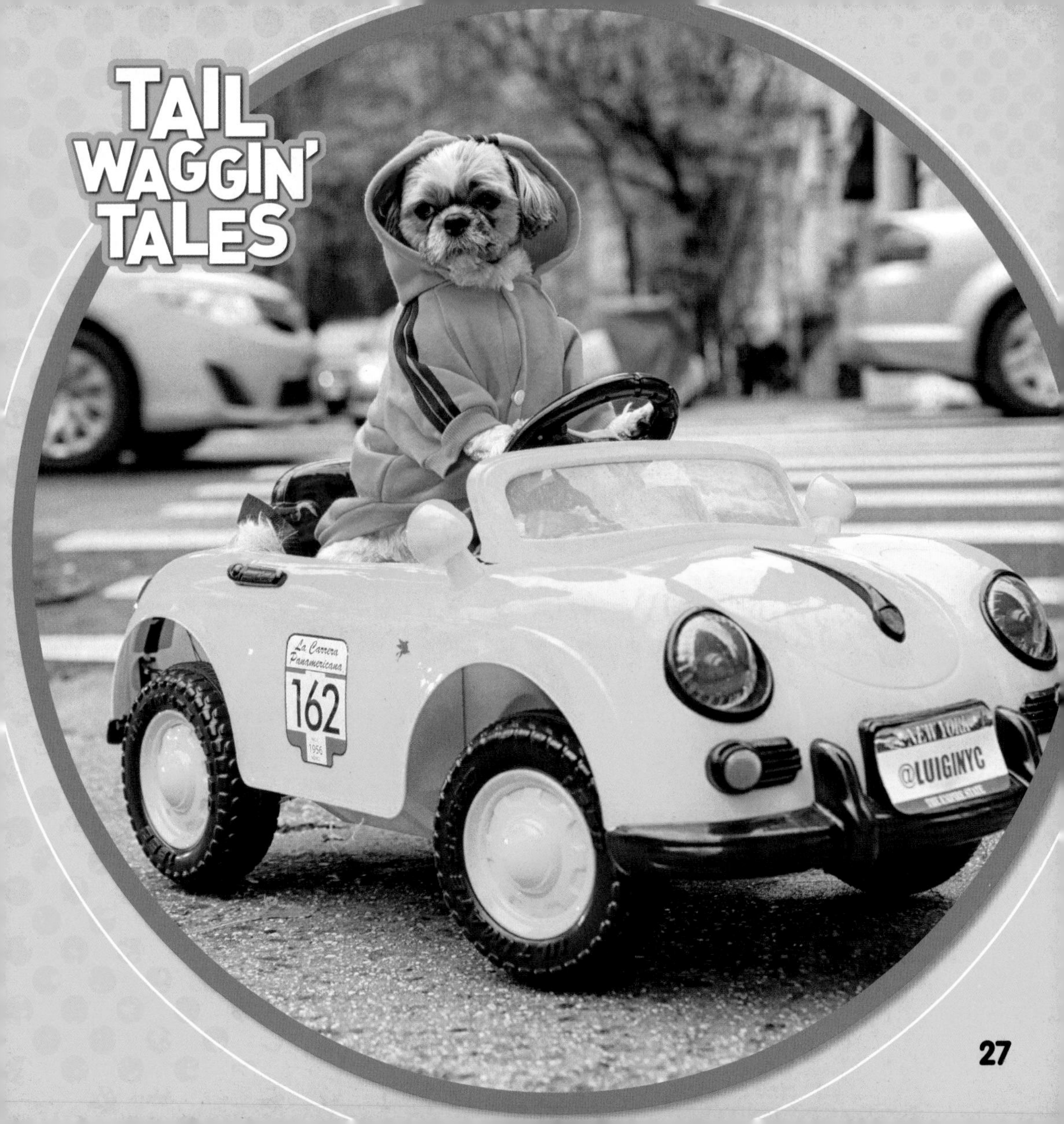

Q

Who was the greatest dog detective?

A

Sherlock Bones.

NAME **Mr. Barkley**

FAVORITE ACTIVITY
Working like a dog

FAVORITE HANGOUT
The office water bowl

PET PEEVE
When the Wi-Fido goes out

I'M HAVING A RUFF DAY AT THE PAW-FFICE.

Q
Where do dogs never shop?
A
At flea markets.
Q
Why did the dog cross the road?
A
Because she was chasing the chicken.
Q
What do you get if you cross a miniature schnauzer and a lion?
A
I'm not sure, but your mail carrier will definitely stop delivering to your house.
Q
What does a dog get when she finishes obedience school?
A
Her pet-degree.

HA! HA! HA! HA!
March 23 is National Puppy Day, a day to celebrate fluffy, slobbery baby balls of love!
KNOCK,
KNOCK.
Who's there?
Pup.
Pup who?
Who ordered the pup-eroni pizza?

Q Why did the dog run in circles on its bed?

A It was trying to catch up on its sleep.

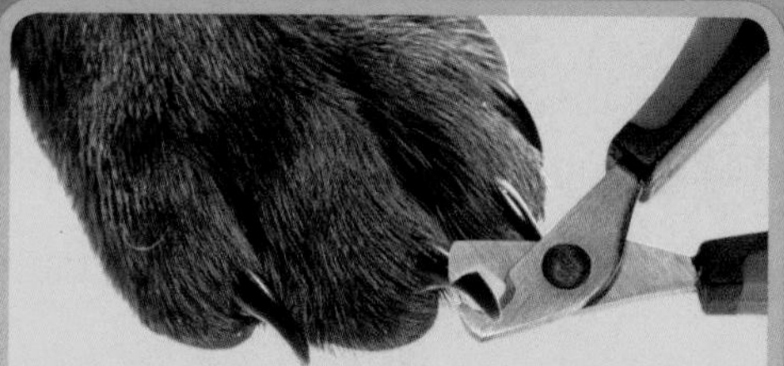

DOG 1: Are you getting your nails cut at the groomers today?

DOG 2: Yes, I am.

DOG 1: Are you sure?

DOG 2: I'm paw-sitive.

The ancient Mesopotamians, Greeks, Romans, and Egyptians made dog collars from leather. The collars were sometimes embellished with gold.

HA! HA! HA! HA! HA! HA! HA! HA!
KNOCK,
KNOCK.
Who's there?
Collar.
Collar who?
Should we just stop by grandma's house or collar first?

TAIL WAGGIN' TALES

NAME: Bodhi the Menswear Dog

BREED: Shiba Inu

FIDO FACTS:

This model pooch may be the most stylish dog in the world. While most furballs aren't let near high-end designer clothing, big brands seek out Bodhi the Menswear Dog for his smouldering good looks. They send him clothing to model! Bodhi, a Shiba Inu, earns his kibble by dressing and posing for his clients and for his social media followers. It started when his humans, Yena Kim and Dave Fung, dressed him up and took pictures on a lazy Saturday. Bodhi really took to it. So Yena and Dave started up a blog called the Menswear Dog. Not long after, Bodhi's gorgeous face made a buzz in the fashion world. This dapper quadruped's owners are now working on a doggie fashion line with a portion of the profits going to animal rescues. This is one floof who can strike a pose!

Bodhi "lights up" when he wears a suit. Still, his humans claim it can take up to 250 shots to get one perfect image.

Bodhi has been featured in major publications, such as *GQ* and the *New York Times.*

Bodhi often receives invitations to weddings all over the world.

Q

What do dog bakers make?

A

Pup-cakes.

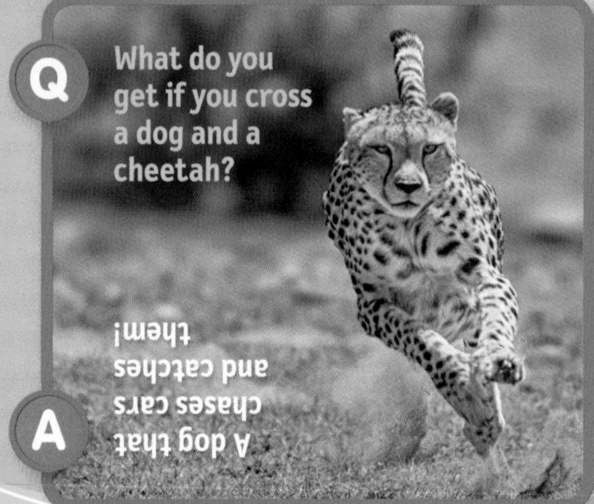

Q

What do you get if you cross a dog and a cheetah?

A

A dog that chases cars and catches them!

Snoopy, the "Peanuts" cartoon dog, is a beagle—a breed known for its intelligence, musical bark, and big, floppy ears!

YORKIE: Ahh! I just saw Dracula's dog!

PUG: What breed was it?

YORKIE: A bloodhound.

Q

What do you get if you cross a **dog** and a **calculator?**

A

A loyal friend you can count on.

A dog's favorite movie characters:

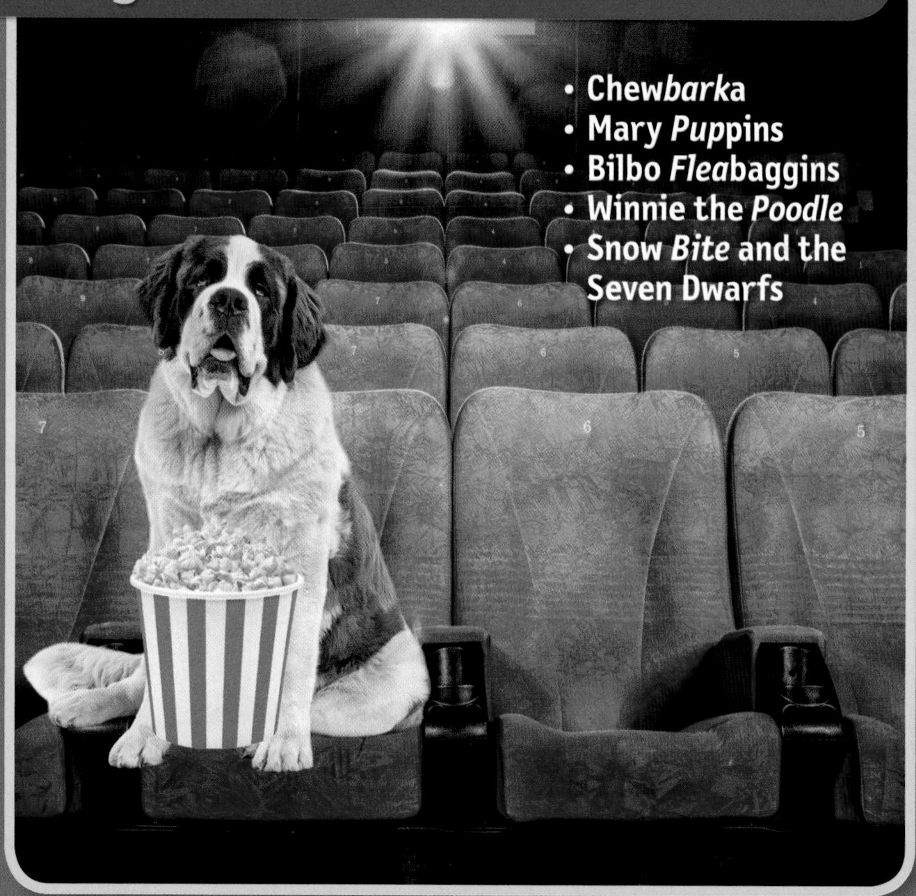

- Chew*bark*a
- Mary *Pup*pins
- Bilbo *Flea*baggins
- Winnie the *Poodle*
- Snow *Bite* and the Seven Dwarfs

New research shows that dogs can tell the difference between a happy person and an angry person.

KNOCK,

KNOCK.

Who's there?

Hugh.

Hugh who?

Hugh's a good dog?!

TEACHER: Your essay called "My Dog" is exactly the same as Luther's. Did you copy him?

VANYA: No ma'am. It's just the same dog.

TONGUE TWISTER!

Say this fast three times:

Willy's wily wiry Weimaraner.

Q What game do dogs play at family picnics?

A Pug-of-war.

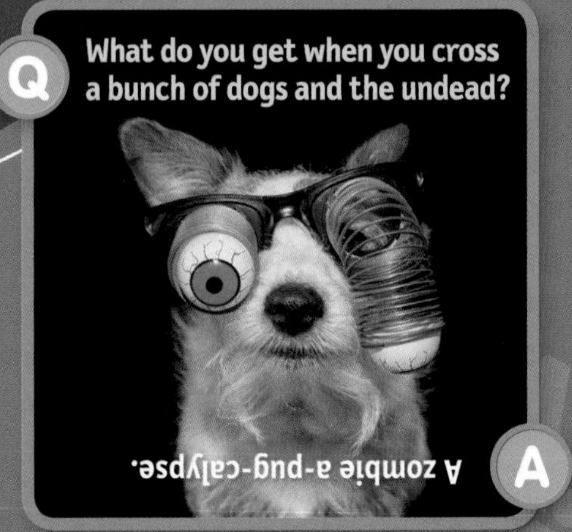

Q What do you get when you cross a bunch of dogs and the undead?

A A zombie a-pug-calypse.

Doberman pinschers were first bred in the 1800s as guard, police, and military dogs.
KNOCK,
KNOCK.
Who's there?
Pinscher.
Pinscher who?
My dinner could use a pinscher two of salt.

PLAYFUL PUPS

NAME Scooter

FAVORITE ACTIVITY
Learning new tricks

FAVORITE HANGOUT
Wherever the pack is

PET PEEVE
Ruff concrete

I'M WHEELY GOOD AT SKATE-BOARDING!

WAITER: How did you enjoy your dinner?

DALMATIAN: It really hit the spots!

Q What do dogs put on top of their sundaes?

A Whippet cream.

Shiba Inus are an ancient dog breed from Japan. "Shiba" means "brushwood" in Japanese, and "inu" means "dog."

TAIL
WAGGIN'
TALES

NAME: Zappa

BREED: Italian greyhound

FIDO FACTS:

Didn't your mother ever tell you not to stick out your tongue? Well, if you were Zappa the Italian greyhound, you wouldn't have been able to help it! After this senior dog lost all but two of her teeth to a dental illness, she couldn't stop her tongue from lolling out of the side of her mouth. But her goofy appearance only increased her cuteness factor! It made the perfect accessory to the many costumes and charming outfits Zappa's owners dressed her up in. Whether it was flapping in the breeze or bundled up in a blanket, Zappa's tongue helped her become an Instagram celebrity with more than 40,000 followers.

Zappa's parents were both show dogs.

Her looks were often compared to Sid the Sloth from the Ice Age movies.

Zappa liked to pal around with her hairless guinea pig besties.

PLAYFUL PUPS

NAME Moochie

FAVORITE ACTIVITY
Eating

FAVORITE FOOD
Whatever I find under the table

PET PEEVE
People who don't share

Q What do you get if you cross a dog and a pasta dish?

A Pughetti.

Q What kind of dog likes heavy metal music?

A A rocker spaniel.

Q What do you get if you cross a dog and a sports car?

A A Lab-orghini.

Q What do puppies call their father's father?

A Grand-paw.

KNOCK,
KNOCK.
Who's there?
Collie.
Collie who?
Do you want me to come over or should I collie you later?
Collies are working dogs originally bred in Scotland to herd sheep.

Dry dog food, in the form of "cakes," was invented in 1860.
KNOCK,
KNOCK.
Who's there?
Kibble.
Kibble who?
Do you have kibble TV?

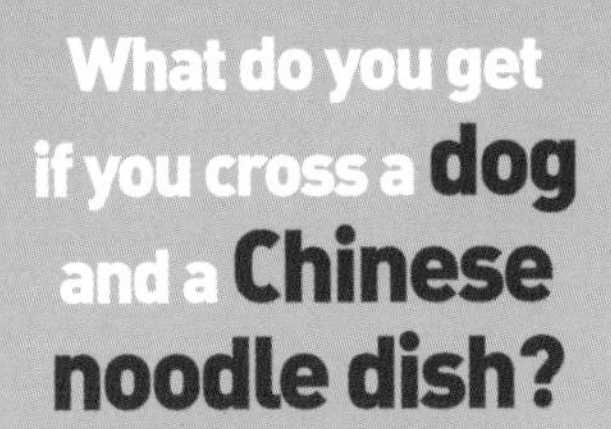

What do you get if you cross a **dog** and a **Chinese noodle dish?**

Chow chow mein.

DOG OWNER: I caught my dog eating the dictionary today!

FRIEND: Did you stop her?

DOG OWNER: Yes, I took the words right out of her mouth.

Q
What kind of dog works in a library?
A hush puppy.
A

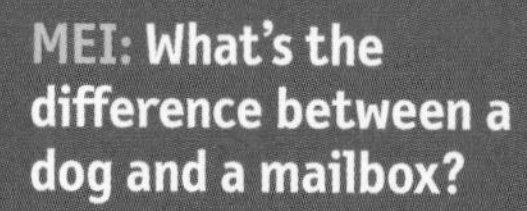

MEI: What's the difference between a dog and a mailbox?

MARIE: I don't know, what?

MEI: Uh ... maybe it's better that I mail my own letters then.

Q Where does a 300-pound mastiff sleep?

A Anywhere it wants to.

Airedales are the largest of the terriers, weighing a hefty 50 to 70 pounds (23–32 kg). They served as messenger and guard dogs during World War I.

Why do dachshunds make terrible bosses?
Because they hound their employees.
Which fruit is fluffy, cute, and has hundreds of red seeds?
A Pomergranian.
In which month do dogs bark the least?
February … it's the shortest month.
What did the puppy order at the coffee shop?
A *pugkin* spice latte.

DOGGONE FUNNY
DID SOMEONE SAY BATH-TIME?

NAME Chomper

HOBBY
Woodworking

FAVORITE HANGOUT
The hardware store

PET PEEVE
Splinters

UM ...
I CAN
EXPLAIN ...

Dogs that have gone down in history:

- *Bark* Obama—howl to the chief!
- Andy War*howl*—his art is pawsitively beautiful
- The Great *Hound*ini—makes all cats disappear
- *Fuzz* Aldrin—first dog to walk, sit, and shake a paw on the moon
- *Drool*ius Caesar—ruler of the doggie day care

Q What did the skeleton say to his dog at dinner time?

A "Bone appétit!"

A dog's superior sense of smell allows them to take in a lot of scents from a car window.

PLAYFUL PUPS

I THINK I NEED A BIGGER WATER BOWL.
NAME Bubbles
FAVORITE ACTIVITY
Soaking in the bath
FAVORITE HANGOUT
The local watering hole
PET PEEVE
Running out of bubbles

Q How many hairs are in a dog's tail?

A None, they are all on the outside.

Q What kind of dog makes the best friend?

A A Pal-matian.

Q How do shih tzus eat spaghetti?

A With their mouths.

Q What is a toy poodle's favorite sport?

A Miniature golf.

HA! HA! HA! HA!
Dingoes are wild dogs native to Australia. They are strong and fast.
KNOCK,
KNOCK.
Who's there?
Dingo.
Dingo who?
The car dingo—there must be engine trouble.

NAME: Bullseye

BREED: Mini English bull terrier

FIDO FACTS:

Bullseye (aka The Target Dog) is a miniature English bull terrier with maximum personality! Bullseye is best known as the mascot for the Target Corporation, appearing in commercials, displays, and ads—but that's not all. This pooch has become a pop culture icon! Whether its walking the red carpet at movie premieres, canoodling with celebrities, or attending Indy car races in a custom racing suit, this dog is living the high life! The pup was even immortalized in the famous Madame Tussauds wax museum in New York City. Bullseye travels with a hair and makeup team that applies the red-and-white bull's-eye target to the dog's face. Not a bad gig for a pooch!

Bullseye's collar sports a custom-made rhinestone bull's-eye dog tag.

Bullseye has a closet full of custom-made costumes, including a tuxedo.

The red, vegetable-based paint used for the bull's-eye is approved by the American Humane Association.

TAIL WAGGIN' TALES

GARY: Why do dogs drink out of the toilet?

EWAN: My mom says it's because the water is colder.

GARY: Ew, how did your mom figure that out?

Q What did one dog say when introduced to another?

A "Howl do you do?"

HA! HA! HA!
KNOCK,
KNOCK.
Who's there?
Canine.
Canine who?
Canine or 10 of my friends come in, too?
Old dogs with graying faces are nicknamed "sugarfaces" because they are sweet and white like sugar.

GET UP! GET UP! IT'S TIME TO GO FOR A WALK!

DOGGONE FUNNY
NO WAY. I'M DOG TIRED.

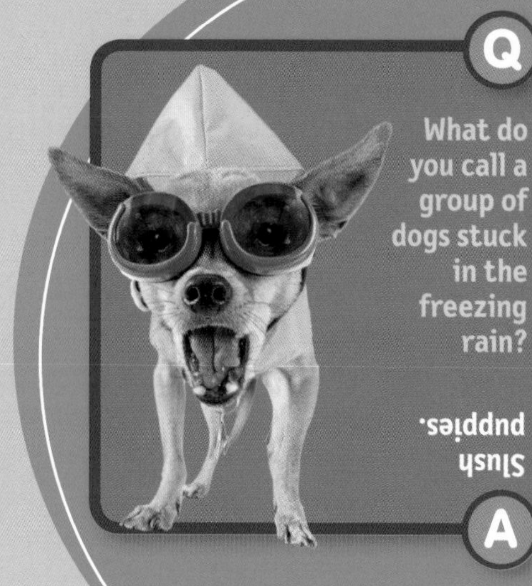

Q What do you call a group of dogs stuck in the freezing rain?

A Slush puppies.

TONGUE TWISTER!

Say this fast three times:

Susie's saluki sips soup and sushi.

Q What do you get if you cross a guard dog and a bird?

A A Doberman fincher.

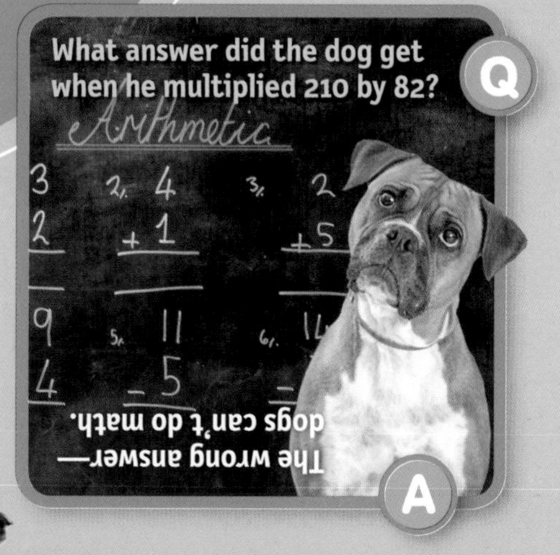

Q What answer did the dog get when he multiplied 210 by 82?

A The wrong answer—dogs can't do math.

KNOCK,
KNOCK.
Who's there?
Tail.
Tail who?
Tail me the password! I want to come in!
Coyotes are North American canine cousins of domestic dogs and wild wolves.

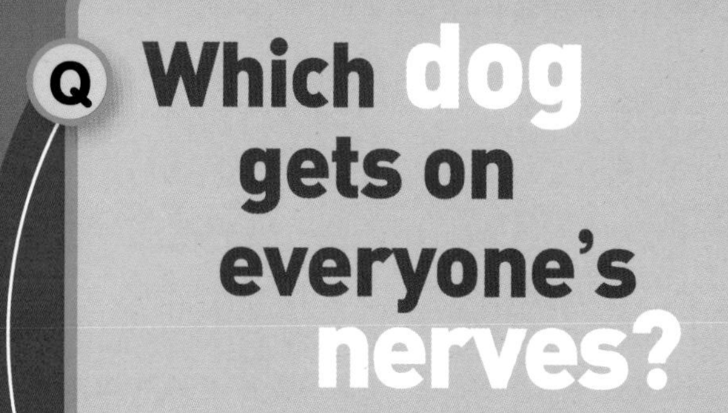

Q **Which dog gets on everyone's nerves?**

A A Great Pain.

BEAGLE: Are you finished picking up all your dog toys yet?

BEAGLE PUPPY: I'll do it later. Quit hounding me!

Why dogs are like social media:

- Like = tail wag
- Post = peeing on hydrants for everyone to sniff
- Friending = sniffing butts
- Sharing = dog hair on EVERYTHING

KNOCK,
KNOCK.
Who's there?
Breed.
Breed who?
Have you got any breed? I want to make a sandwich.
Known for their intelligence and loyalty, German shepherds are often trained as police and guard dogs.

Q **What kind of dog always needs a shave?**

A A bearded collie.

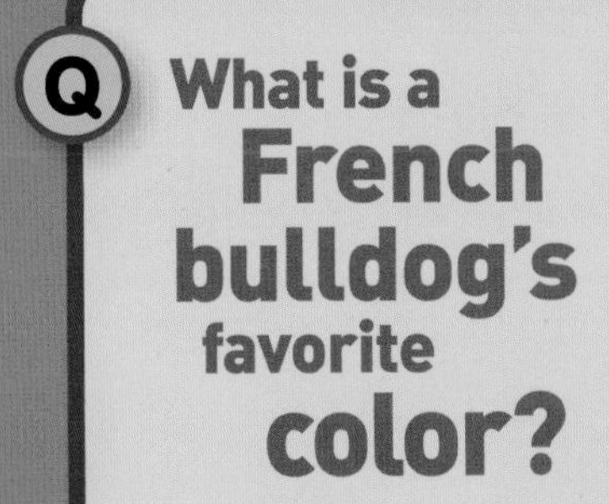

Q **What is a French bulldog's favorite color?**

A Grrrr-een.

Q
What did the basset hound think of the fancy hotel?
He said it was very paw-sh.
A

RECEPTION

HA! HA! HA! HA! HA! HA! HA!
KNOCK,
KNOCK.
Who's there?
Theodore.
Theodore who?
Theodore is closed, and the dog needs to go out.
Dalmatians are born without spots. They only gain spots as they age.

Q

What is the Dalmatian's website address?

A

Dog-dot-dot-dot-dot-dot-dot-dot-com.

DOG OWNER: I'm worried my dog is upset.

VET: Why do you think that?

DOG OWNER: Because when I asked him how his day was he said "ruff."

Q Why did the Lhasa apso put her bed on the chandelier?

A Because she was a light sleeper.

Q What do you get if you cross a large dog and a bottle of perfume?

A A Scent Bernard.

Q What kind of soda do dogs drink?

A Pup-si Cola.

Q Which dog sweats the most?

A A hot-weiler.

HA! HA! HA! HA!
KNOCK,
KNOCK.
Who's there?
Pointer.
Pointer who?
Are you going to make your pointer not?
German pointer dogs were originally bred for fetching birds for hunters. Their name comes from the way they point their snouts toward prey.

DOGGONE FUNNY
THIS IS THE THIRD HOLE I'VE DUG. WHERE DID I BURY THOSE BONES?

WAITER: Wow! We don't often see dogs eating in this restaurant.

DOG: With these prices, I'm not surprised!

Q

Why is a dog's nose in the middle of its face?

Because it's the scenter.

A

- Pita bull
- Ramen poodles
- Sushiba Inu
- Broccollie
- Puddingo

TAIL
WAGGIN'
TALES

NAME: Scooby

BREED: Great Dane

FIDO FACTS:

He's everybody's favorite talking Great Dane. But then again, are there any others? Scoobert "Scooby" Doo—or "Roobee Roo" as he calls himself—began his crime-solving and ghost-busting career in 1969, appearing in the *Scooby-Doo, Where are You!* Saturday morning television cartoon. And he's been going strong ever since! Despite being a big scaredy-cat, almost every crime solved by Mystery Inc. (the crime-fighting gang of friends he's a member of) is thanks to good ol' Scoob. Where does Scooby get his bravery from? The promise of a Scooby Snack. Lots and lots of Scooby Snacks. He'd do almost anything to get one, even if it means fighting a ghost or chasing down a goblin.

Scooby has a nephew named Scrappy-Doo.

Scooby is a triplet. He has two brothers, Skippy-Doo and Yabba-Doo.

There are 12 different Scooby-Doo cartoon series, two live-action movies, 21 video games, and 25 DVD movies.

TONGUE TWISTER!

Say this fast three times:

The bichon frise sees cheese.

Q Which dog can you see in the dark?

A A Glow-berman pinscher.

Q What's the difference between a greyhound and a duck?

A One goes quick and the other goes quack.

Q Why was the dog afraid of math class?

A He didn't want to get arithme-ticks.

Bloodhounds have been used to track humans and other animals for centuries. Their floppy ears and droopy skin make them supercute, too!
KNOCK,
KNOCK.
Who's there?
Hound.
Hound who?
Come out with your hounds up!

PLAYFUL PUPS

WINTER IS SNOW MUCH FUN!
NAME Frosty
FAVORITE ACCESSORY Ear-ruffs
FAVORITE ACTIVITY Snow-and-tell
FAVORITE FOOD Chilly dogs

Lesser known breeds:

- Terrierdactyl = extinct breed of yappy, flying dinosaur
- Peagle = a round, green hunting dog
- Hoarder collie = keeps every stick it finds
- Toucanine = brightly colored dog with wings
- Jotterhound = takes very thorough notes

Q

Why did the dad **adopt** a **dachshund** for his **five kids?**

He wanted a dog they could all pet at once.

A

A group of pugs is called a grumble.

Q What do you put on a fluffy dog to help its hair grow?

A Fur-tilizer.

RIZZO: My dog doesn't have a nose.

ACE: How does he smell?

RIZZO: Not too bad, he just had a bath.

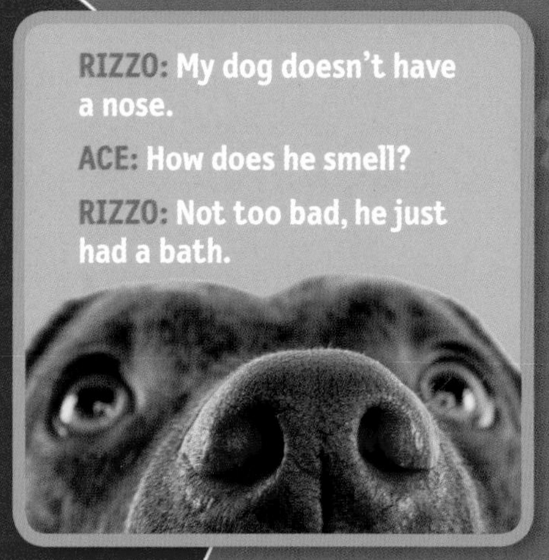

Q How do you see a Dalmatian in the dark?

A With a spotlight.

Q What do you get if you cross a border collie and a lamb?

A A sheep that can round itself up.

HA! HA! HA! HA! HA!
Jackals yip and howl instead of barking.
KNOCK,
KNOCK.
Who's there?
Bark.
Bark who?
I brought kibble for the bark-becue.

Q

What kind of car do dogs ride in when they are sick?

A

A Cor-vet.

CARMEN:
My dog once caught a ball that was 10 feet in the air.
CHARLOTTE:
That seems far-fetched.

Q
What kind of dog loves playing in the snow?
A
A Saint Brrrrr-nard.

Bull terriers are the clowns of the dog world. They are playful and goofy.

Q

When is a dog like a baseball game?

A

When it chases fowls.

Q

What do you get if you cross a tall dog and a pastry?

A

A Great Dane-ish.

DOGGONE FUNNY
IT'S GOING TO RAIN CATS AND DOGS TODAY.
HA! HA!

Q

What is **brown, gray,** and has **eight legs** and a **trunk?**

A

A chocolate Lab on vacation with an elephant.

TONGUE TWISTER!

Say this fast three times:

A boy fed his Samoyed.

Q

What kind of cheese do dogs get on their pizza?

A

Mutts-arella.

PIZZA PIZZA
PIZZA PIZZA
PIZZA PIZZA

Q

Where do dogs buy their underwear?

A

At K9-Mart.

Q
What do you call a dog that can breathe underwater?
Scuba-Doo.
A
HA! HA!

DOGGONE FUNNY

WHERE DOES SHE PUT ALL OF HER STUFF?

Q
What kind of dog should you have around when it's chilly?
A
An Afghan.
Q
What kind of quizzes are dogs good at?
A
Lab tests.

According to legend, a pug saved the life of Holland's Prince of Orange by barking loudly when his camp was under attack by Spanish troops.

NAME: Doug the Pug

BREED: Pug

FIDO FACTS:

He's just a pug living a pug life ... and making people deliriously happy along the way. Doug the Pug is the world's most famous pug—a KING in fact—according to his own biography: *Doug the Pug: King of Pop Culture*. Wait a minute! A pepperoni-pizza-eating pup is the king of pop culture? Yip! Doug doesn't mind barking up his own tree. He's got millions of social media followers and a host of celebrity friends. But not so long ago, Doug was just an ordinary dog hanging out on the couch with his owner Leslie Mosier. Leslie decided the world needed a dose of Doug's adorable cuteness, and—voilà—a pop culture king was born! In a shower cap, in costumes, in snuggly pj's, Doug's perfect posing is a feast for the eyes. Now that's a good boy!

Doug has appeared in several music videos with big-time stars.

Doug hails from Nashville, Tennessee, U.S.A.

This funny pooch has his own line of stuffies, posters, and books.

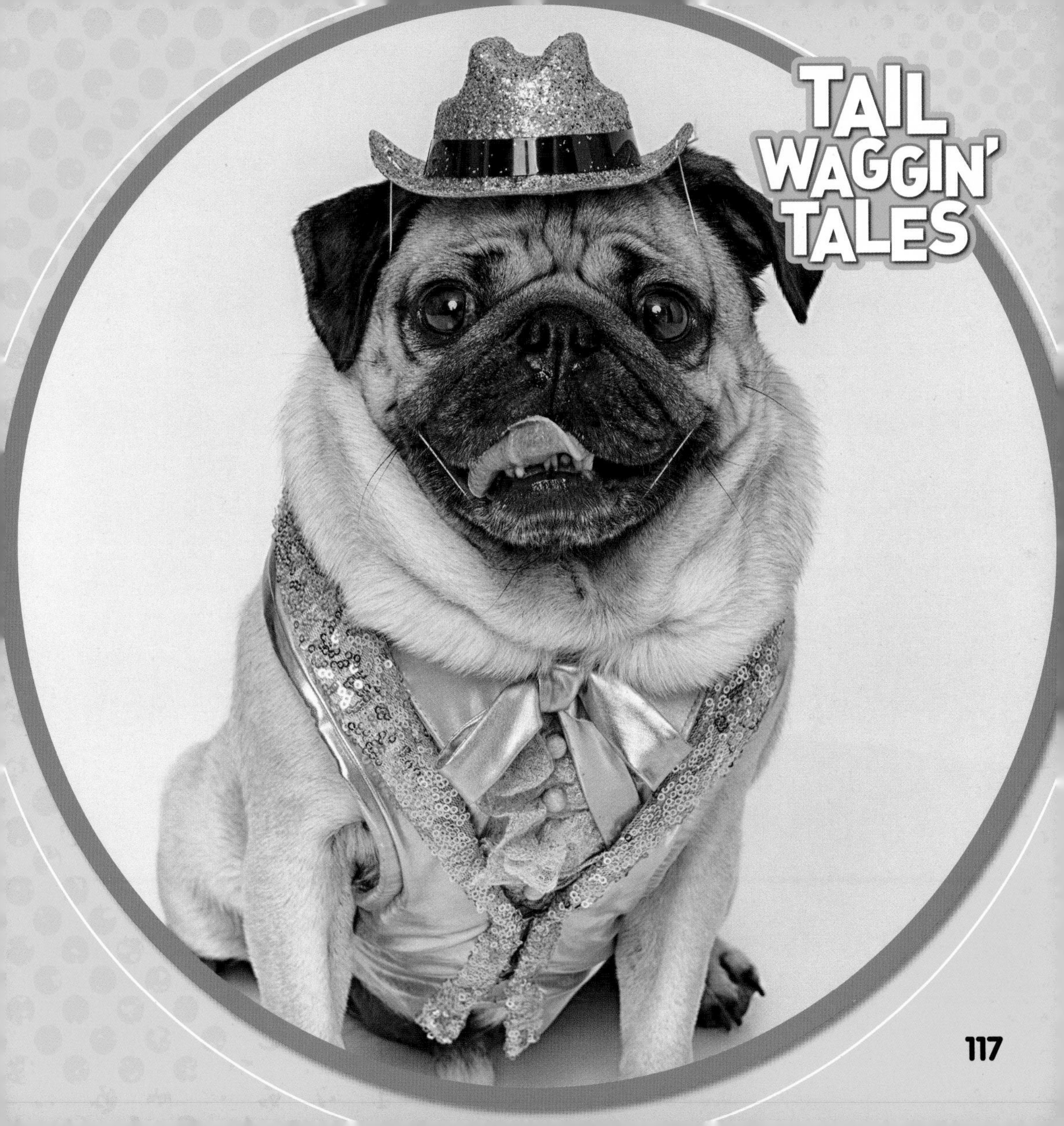

Q
What's worse than one dog barking at the mail carrier?
A
Two dogs barking at the mail carrier.
VET: Your dog needs her ears cleaned.
DOG OWNER: I want a second opinion.
VET: OK, she's also really cute.
Q
Why did the bulldogs get married?
A
They found each other fetching.
Q
Why do dogs scratch themselves?
A
Because they are the only ones that know where it itches.

Kennel clubs are groups that promote the care and breeding of dogs. Some kennel clubs organize dog shows!
KNOCK,
KNOCK.
Who's there?
Kennel.
Kennel who?
Kennel tell you the funniest joke!

DOGGONE FUNNY

THIS SOCK IS NO MATCH FOR CHEWTON THE DESTROYER! EATER OF LOST SOCKS!

Q
Why was the cairn terrier kicked out of the butcher shop?
A
He was caught chop-lifting.
Q
What do you get if you cross a poodle and a kangaroo?
A
A dog with somewhere to put its own leash.
Q
Which dog tells boring stories?
A
The Dull-matian.
Q
Where do herding dogs live?
A
In Collie-fornia.

HA! HA! HA!
KNOCK,
KNOCK.
Who's there?
Corgi.
Corgi who?
You are corgi-lly invited to my birthday party.
Queen Elizabeth II is probably the world's most famous corgi lover. She is believed to have had 30 of the short-legged dogs over her lifetime.

Who is a dog's favorite composer?

Ludwig van Barkhoven.

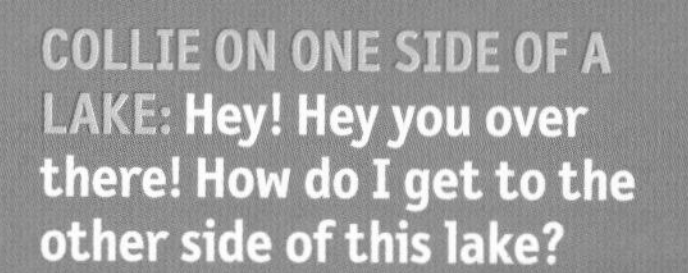

COLLIE ON ONE SIDE OF A LAKE: **Hey! Hey you over there! How do I get to the other side of this lake?**

WHIPPET ON THE OTHER SIDE OF THE LAKE: **You ARE on the other side of the lake!**

Q

What's black and white and barks at hockey players?

A

The rufferee.

HA! HA! HA!
KNOCK,
KNOCK.
Who's there?
Bow.
Bow who?
No, silly, it's
bow WOW.
Labrador retrievers are the most popular dogs in the United States, but they were originally bred to be water dogs in Newfoundland and Labrador, Canada.

Jobs for dogs:

- Barktic explorer
- Pugkin farmer
- Puparazzi
- Accorgian player
- Pawdyguard
- Roof-er

REX: Do we still have to go to obedience class tonight?

BUDDY: Nope. School is rover for the day.

Q

What is a basset hound's favorite food?

A

Whatever is on your plate.

Siberian huskies are descendants of pack and sled animals kept by the Chukchi people of the Arctic and northeastern Asia.
KNOCK,
KNOCK.
Who's there?
Arf.
Arf who?
Arf we going to the park?

Q What do dog bakers use to make bread?

A Fi-dough.

Say this fast three times:

The whippet weathered wetter weather better.

Q What kind of terrier can jump higher than a building?

A Any kind—buildings can't jump.

Q What do dogs eat at the movie theatre?

A Pupcorn.

What do Austrian composer Wolfgang Amadeus Mozart and British Queen Victoria have in common? They loved tiny, fluffy Pomeranian pups!
KNOCK, KNOCK.
Who's there?
Pooch.
Pooch who?
Pooch your shoes on. We're going out!

I'M PRETENDING I'M A DOGWOOD TREE!
DOGGONE FUNNY

I THINK I WET MY PLANTS.
I'M A COLLIE-FLOWER!

Q Why does a dog wag its tail?

A No one else will do it for them.

Q What do you order at a dog café?

A Coffee and a beagle.

Q **What did the dog say to the tree?**

A "Bark."

Q **Why did the Dalmatian hide in the bushes?**

A To avoid being spotted.

KNOCK,
KNOCK.
Who's there?
Sara.
Sara who?
Sara puppy in there with you?
Chihuahuas are descendants of ancient Aztec dogs called techichis.

TAIL
WAGGIN'
TALES

NAME: Manny the Frenchie

BREED: French bulldog

FIDO FACTS:

Bonjour! Meet Manny the Frenchie. He may not actually be French, but he is a French bulldog ... the "World's Most Followed Bulldog" to be specific! Manny has more than three million followers on his social media pages. That's the same as the entire population of San Diego, California, U.S.A.! And while posing in funny costumes or rocking a pair of sunglasses is normal for him, his real specialty lies in snoozing. This pupper is photographed catching some z's in the cutest (and strangest) positions and places. One of his favorite places to nap? The bathroom sink. Good thing the tap doesn't leak!

Manny's favorite treat is bacon.

Manny is a *paw*thor! His book, *Manny the Frenchie's Art of Happiness*, offers tips on how to live your best life.

Manny uses his overwhelming popularity to run a foundation that supports animal and human causes.

Q
What do you call it when a greyhound can't catch a rabbit?
A
A bad hare day.
PUG: How did you enjoy dinner?
DALMATIAN: It really hit the spot.
Q
What do you call a short dog dressed in camouflage?
A
In-corg-nito.
Q
What do you call a shar-pei that's been in the sun all day?
A
A hot dog.

Q

Which dog hangs out at salons?

A

A shampoodle.

PUPS

MY FAVORITE YOGA POSE IS DOWNWARD DOG.

NAME **Gym**

FAVORITE DINOSAUR
Tricera-squats

FAVORITE SAYING
“Good things come to those who weight.”

PET PEEVE
Missing leg day

DOG 1: Is the vet going to weigh you today?

DOG 2: Yes, I can't weight!

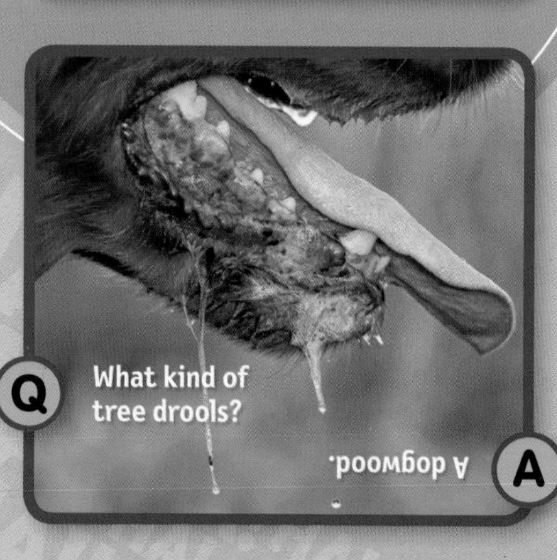

Q What kind of tree drools?

A A dogwood.

The dachshund's long body has earned it the nicknames "sausage dog" and "wiener dog."

Shar-pei means "sand skin" in Chinese. It refers to the dog's rough, bristle-like coat.

Q

What kind of dog digs up ancient treasures?

A

A bark-eologist.

Q

What do dogs have that no other animals have?

A

Puppies.

Q

What did the groomer say to the dog?

A

"Long time no flea!"

Q

What do lazy dogs chase?

A

Parked cars.

PLAYFUL PUPS

PUP, PUP, AND AWAY!

NAME Pilot Scraps

FAVORITE SAYING
"This is just plane awesome."

FAVORITE HANGOUT
The airplane hanger

PET PEEVE
Jet lag

Q

What is a corgi's favorite dessert?

A

Strawberry shortcake.

Say this fast three times:

A big black boxer on a big black rug.

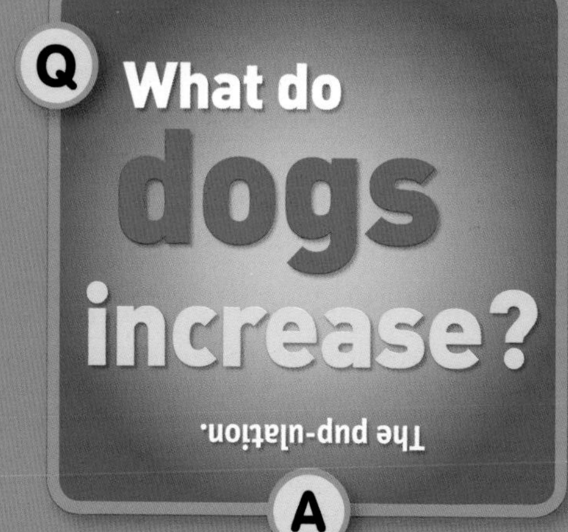

Q

What do dogs increase?

A

The pup-ulation.

MOVIE THEATER USHER: Excuse me, sir. Why is your dog watching this movie?

MOVIEGOER: I don't know—he hated the book.

It's hard to believe it, but tiny six-pound (2.7-kg) Pomeranians are descended from sled dogs from Iceland and Lapland.
KNOCK,
KNOCK.
Who's there?
Patty.
Patty who?
Patty dog on the head or scratch her ears. She loves it.

I WILL BE A GOOD BOY. I WILL BE A GOOD BOY. I WILL BE A GOOD BOY.

PLAYFUL PUPS

NAME Chicken!

FAVORITE SNACK
Chicken!

FAVORITE PASTIME
Chicken!

PET PEEVE
Not eating chicken!

Q When is a stray dog most likely to enter a house?

A When the door is open.

Q Why is a big tree like a yappy dog?

A They both have a lot of bark.

Dogs have about 300 smell receptors that help them detect smells as they travel through the air.

HA! HA! HA!
Q
What do you get if you cross an amphibian and a hunting dog?
A
A croaker spaniel.
Q
What do you call a red-haired dog on a plane?
A
A jet-setter!
HA! HA! HA!

I'll have a Havanese, please! These fluffy pooches were first bred on the Caribbean island of Cuba.

DOGGONE FUNNY

WE LOOK FRIGHTFULLY GOOD! I'M SO GLAD WE STOPPED AT THAT BOO-TIQUE.

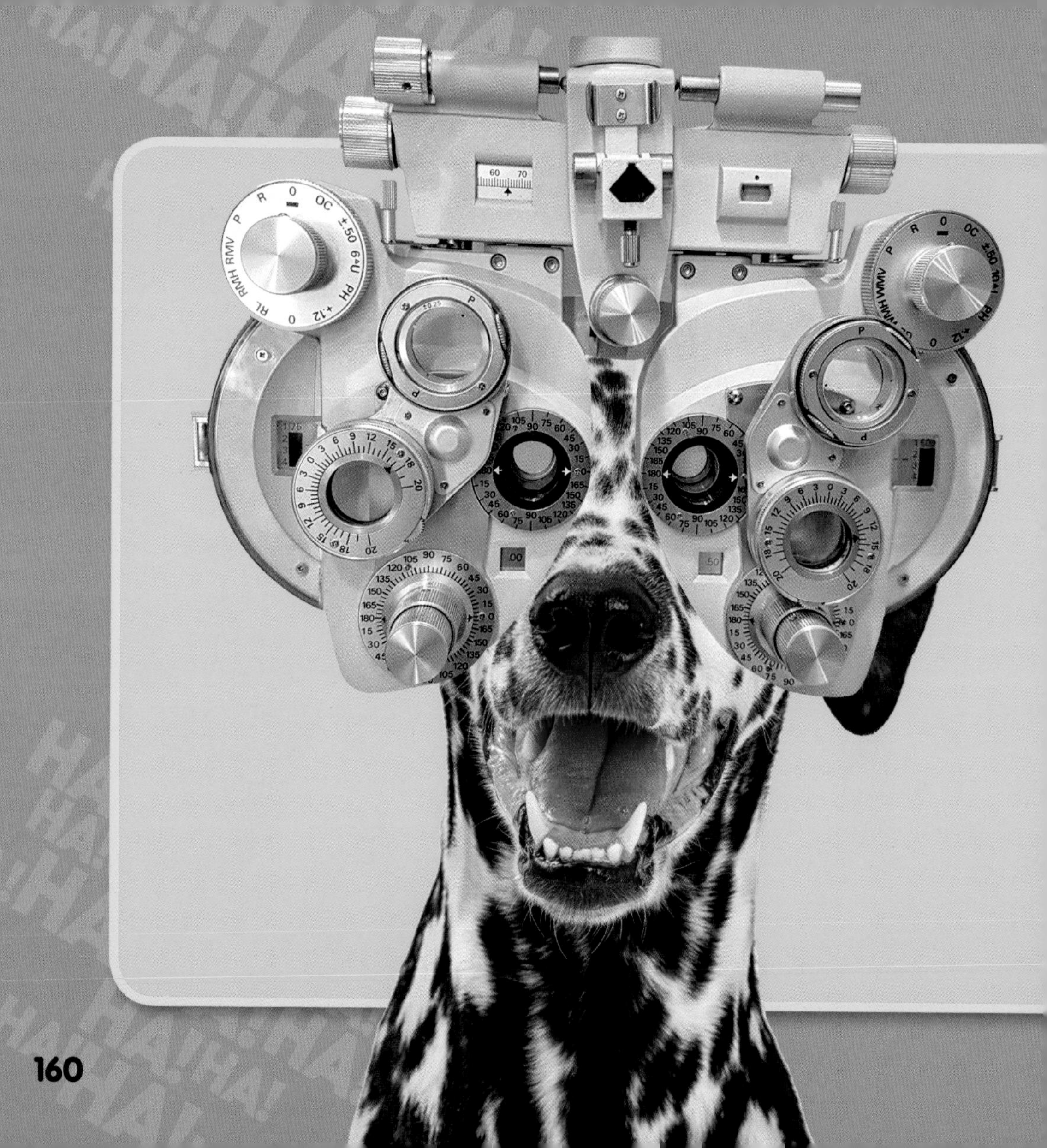

Q

Why did the Dalmatian go to the eye doctor?

He was seeing spots.

A

Q

When is a dog's tail not a tail?

A When it's a waggin'.

DOG OWNER: Help! My dog ate the TV remote.

VET: No problem. I'll be right over to help.

DOG OWNER: What do I do in the meantime?

VET: Read a book.

With their keen sense of smell, Irish setters are excellent at helping hunters find and retrieve game birds.

HA! HA! HA! HA! HA! HA!

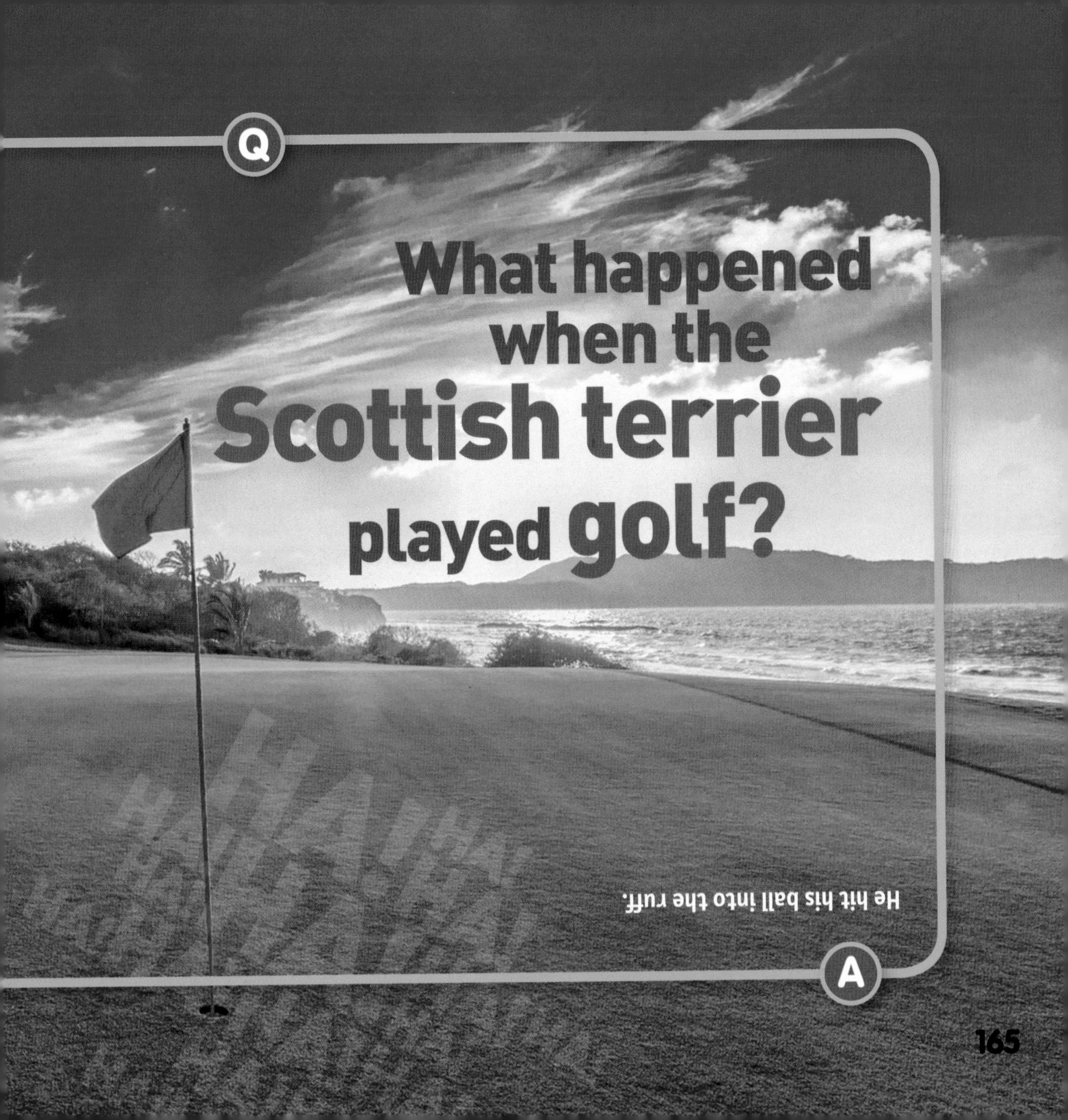

Q

What happened when the Scottish terrier played golf?

He hit his ball into the ruff.

A

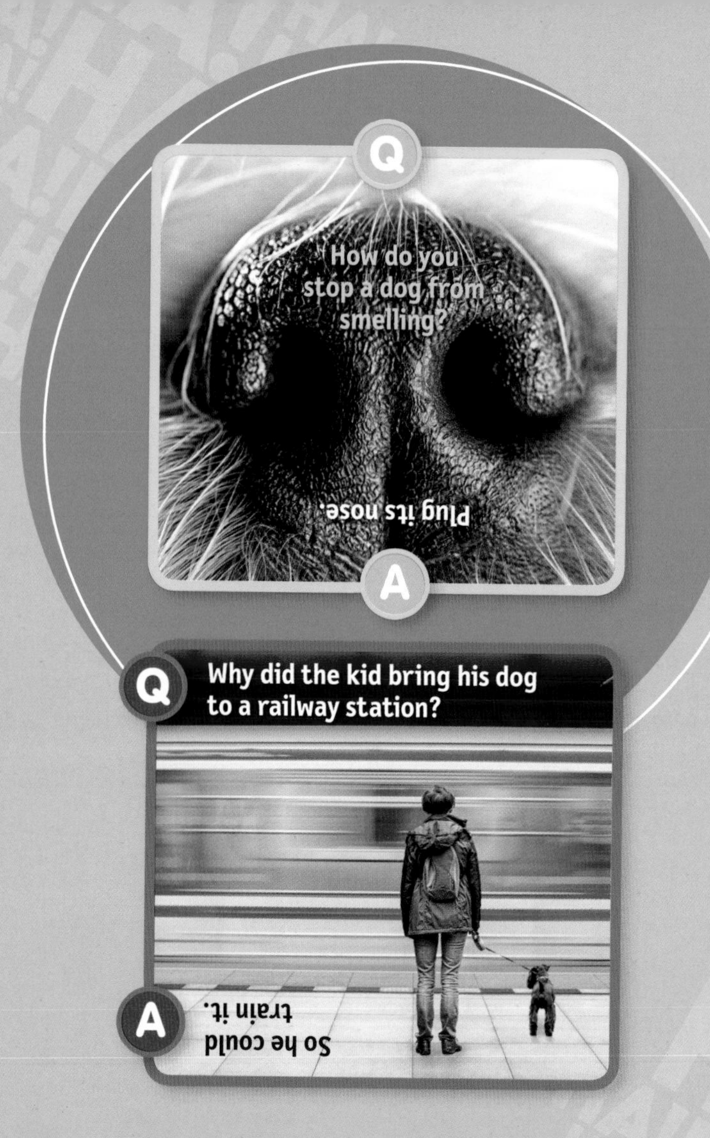
Q
How do you stop a dog from smelling?
A
Plug its nose.
Q
Why did the kid bring his dog to a railway station?
A
So he could train it.

HA! HA! HA! HA! HA! HA!
Bulldogs are famous mascots; 39 American universities use the pudgy toughies to represent their schools.
KNOCK,
KNOCK.
Who's there?
Paws.
Paws who?
I need to paws and catch my breath.

HEY! SAVE SOME FOR US!

DOGGONE FUNNY

I GOT IT! I GOT IT! I KNEW THESE EARS WOULD COME IN HANDY!
DOGGONE FUNNY

Q
What do you get if you cross a small, furry dog and a large boat?
A ship tzu.
A

Q
Why did the dog cross the road twice?
She was trying to fetch a boomerang.
A

Q When is a black dog not a black dog?

A When it's a greyhound.

MARCUS: I bought my pooch a dog whistle.

LOUISE: Does it work?

MARCUS: I don't know. He won't use it.

Q Where did the terrier leave its car?

A The barking lot.

Q What's a dog's favorite hobby?

A Collecting fleas.

The Afghan hound is one of the world's oldest dog breeds. They have been around since 2200 B.C.
KNOCK,
KNOCK.
Who's there?
Afghan.
Afghan who?
I've gone as far as Afghan.

DOGGONE FUNNY

I'M SO COLD! I GUESS THAT MAKES ME A CHILI DOG!

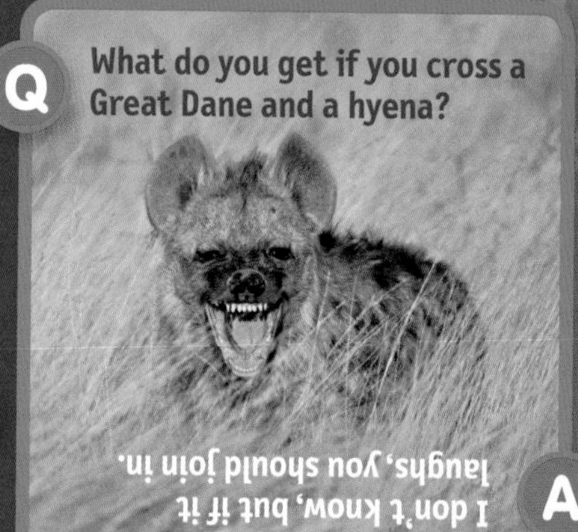

TONGUE TWISTER!

Say this fast three times:

If a dog chews shoes, whose shoes does she choose?

HA! HA! HA! HA! HA!

A German wirehaired pointer's dense coat is almost completely water repellent.

Q

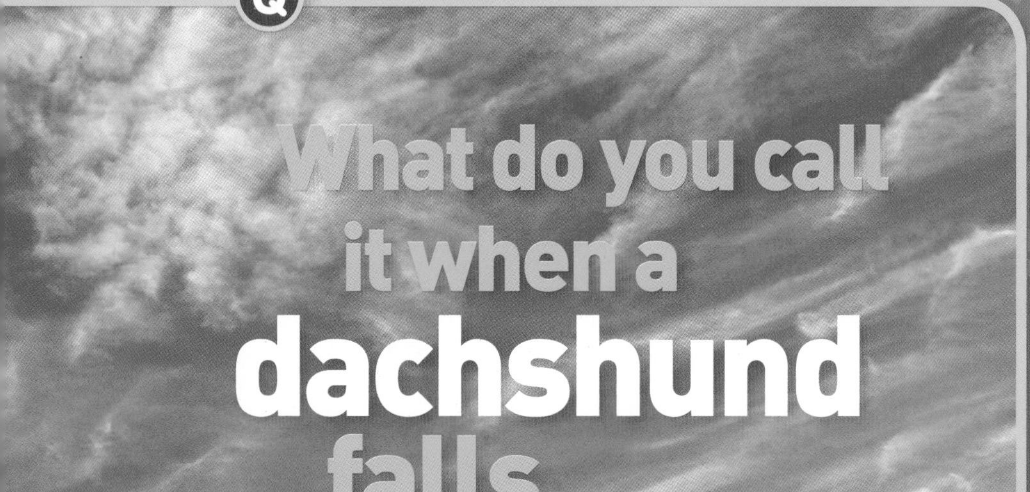

What do you call it when a dachshund falls down a hill?

A

A sausage roll.

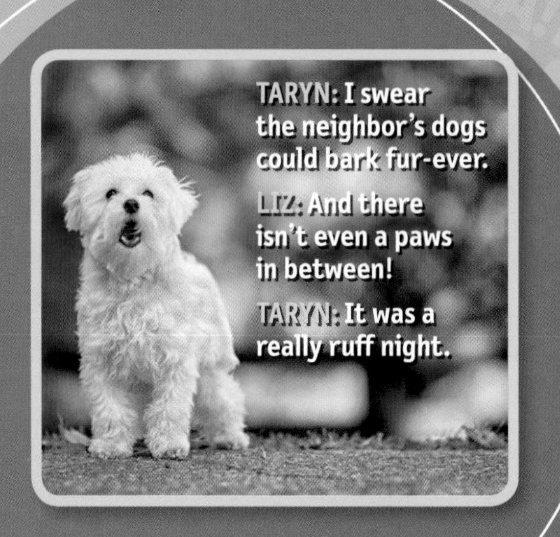
TARYN: I swear the neighbor's dogs could bark fur-ever.
LIZ: And there isn't even a paws in between!
TARYN: It was a really ruff night.

Q
What do you get when you cross a dog with an Olympic sprinter?
A
The 100-yard dash-hund.

Great Danes can weigh up to 175 pounds (79 kg).
KNOCK,
KNOCK.
Who's there?
Ruff.
Ruff who?
My dog is having a ruff time in obedience class.

NAME: Ramsey the Blue Staffy

BREED: Staffordshire bull terrier

FIDO FACTS:

He's bold, blue, and a bodacious ambassador for his breed. He's Ramsey the blue staffy, and he's changing the way people view Staffordshire bull terriers one ear-to-ear smile and sloppy kiss at a time. This gentle, loving blue-gray pooch was underweight and limping when we was adopted by his owner in England. Now he's a muscle-bound pupper who poses with his teddy bear on social media. He's proving pic by captivating pic that he and staffies are sweet by nature. Hundreds of thousands of fans agree—Ramsey has captured their attention and their hearts!

The Staffordshire police in England have a staffy police dog named Cooper.

Ramsey's favorite holiday is Halloween. He likes to dress up.

As a pup, Ramsey had blue eyes.

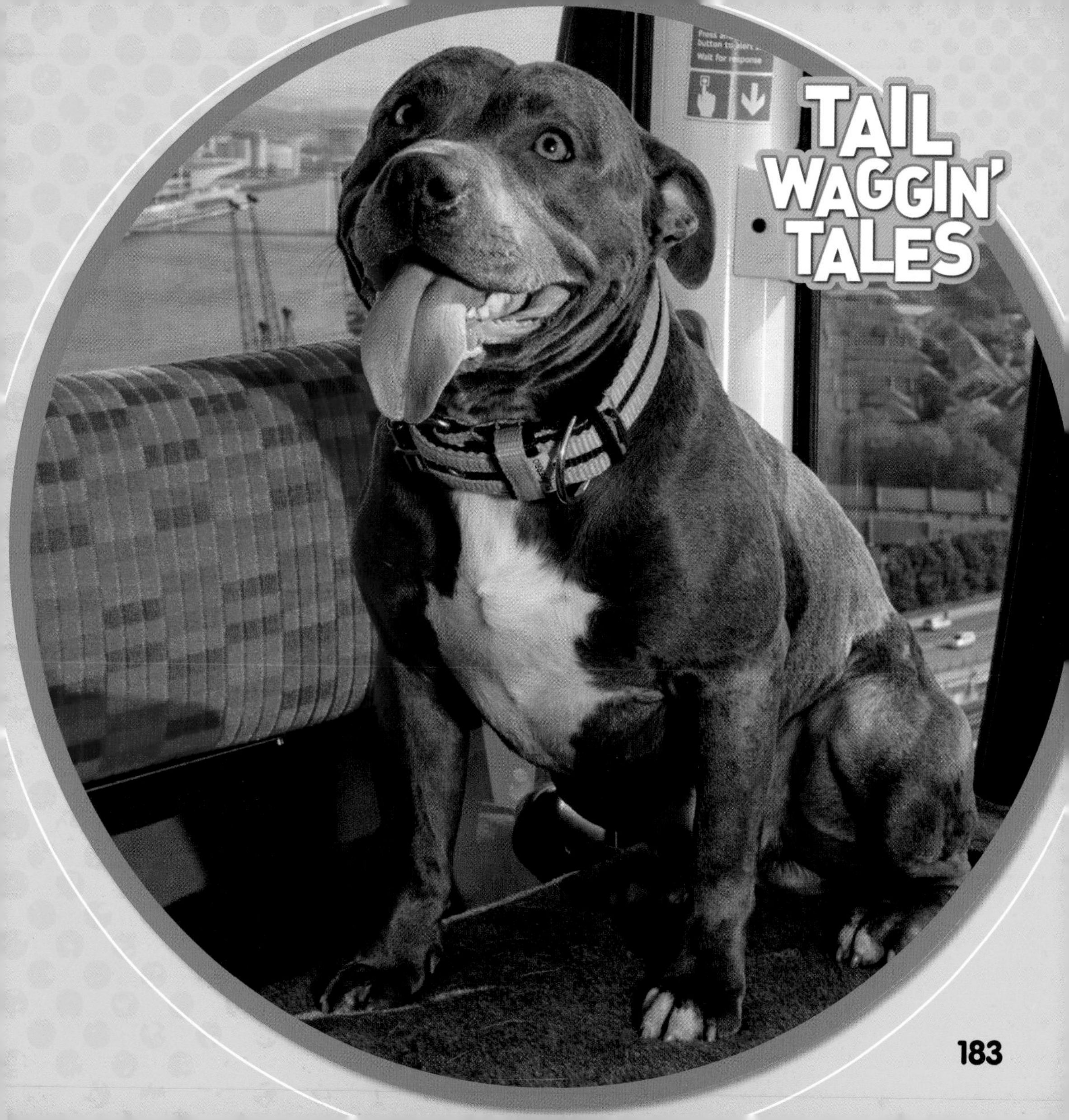

Q

Why did the **lazy kid** adopt a **Great Dane?**

A

So he wouldn't have to bend down to pet it.

TONGUE TWISTER!

Say this fast three times:

Unique Yorkie in New York.

Q

What should you do if you see an angry dog?

A

Hope it doesn't see you.

Q

What's **red,** has 1,000 eyes, 2,000 feet, and **whines?**

A

500 Irish setters begging for a treat.

Adult dogs have 42 teeth—10 more than the average human.

Q How do you find a dog in the woods?

HA! HA!

Q Why do dogs run in circles?

A Because it's hard to run in squares.

Q What do you get if you cross a dog and a cell phone?

A Collar ID.

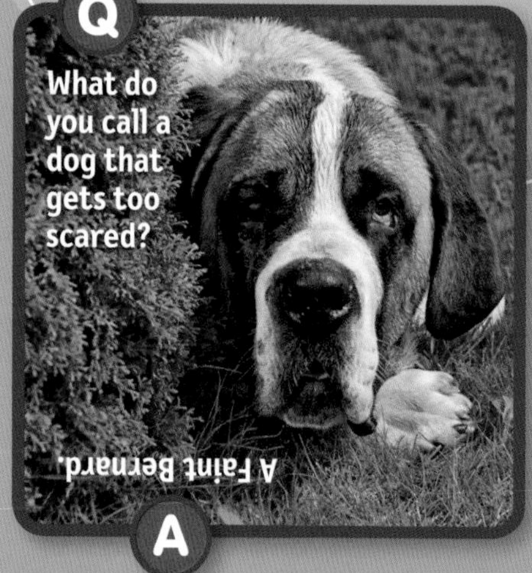

Q What do you call a dog that gets too scared?

A A Faint Bernard.

Q What do you call a dog doctor that fell in a lake?

A A wet-erinarian.

KNOCK,
KNOCK.
Who's there?
Litter.
Litter who?
My dog is tired. Can you litter in?
The record for the largest litter of puppies is held by Tia, a Neapolitan mastiff. She had 24 pups.

DOGGONE FUNNY

WHAT IS THIS, BEEF? I THINK I'M ON THE WRONG SIDE OF THE BOWL.
DOG

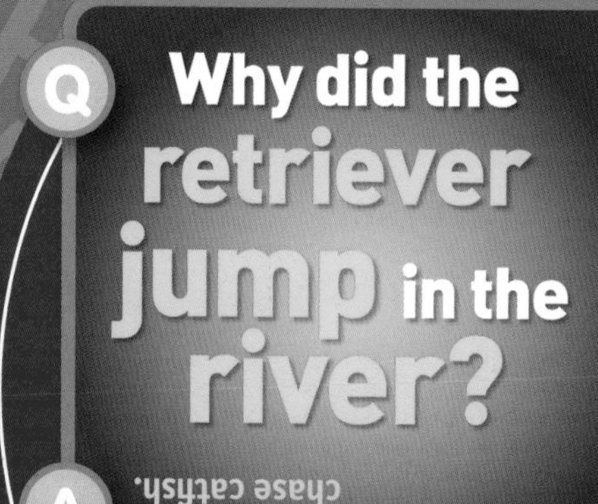

Q Why did the retriever jump in the river?

A So it could chase catfish.

DOG 1: Just thought I'd collie you to say hi.

DOG 2: Are you coming over for the howl-idays?

DOG 1: It's paw-sible! I'm going mutts with excitement!

Q How do dogs from Japan say hello?

A *Konnichihuahua.*

Q What do you do when a Yorkshire terrier sneezes?

A Grab a tiny tissue.

Dogs pant a lot. They pant to cool down because they cannot sweat. They also pant when they are afraid or ill.
KNOCK,
KNOCK.
Who's there?
Arthur.
Arthur who?
Arthur anymore puppies in there?

TAIL WAGGIN' TALES

NAME: Snoopy

BREED: Beagle

FIDO FACTS:

This wacky, wild, and wobbly beagle just might be the most famous dog in the world. And he's a comic! This cheeky pup vibrates with energy. Snoopy sings (not well), dances (with wild abandon), reads (two words a day), and flies a plane (and his doghouse!). Not bad for a line-drawn white-and-black beagle. He's a star in the *Peanuts* comic strip, movies, and television specials. Even with his fame, this pooch still enjoys the simple things in life—like pizza and root beer. Snoopy fans, however, have rewarded him with his own star on the Hollywood Walk of Fame. Now that's loyalty!

Snoopy is as comfortable walking on two legs as he is on four.

Cartoonist Charles M. Schulz based Snoopy on his childhood dog, Spike.

Snoopy has his own sidekick and root-beer-drinking buddy—a messy-headed yellow bird named Woodstock.

Q

What do you get if you cross a guard dog and a boxer?

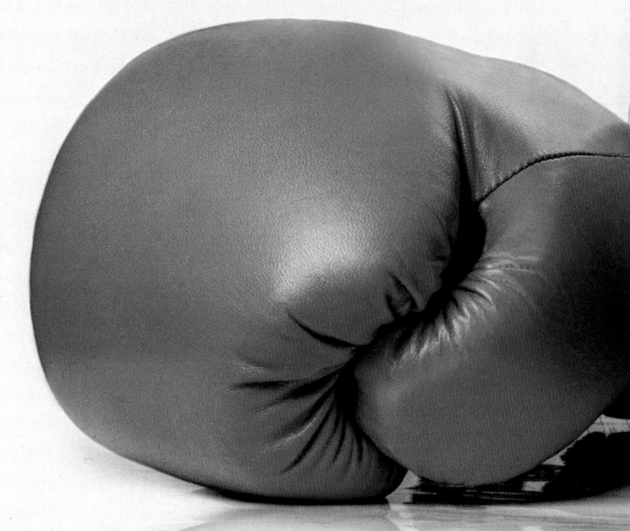

A Doberman puncher.

A

Q
When is a good time to walk a dog?
A
When they leash expect it.
Q
What happened when the bull terrier ate his owner's glasses?
A
He made a spectacle of himself.
HA! HA! HA! HA!

Harriers are a rare breed. There are only around 1,000 of them registered in the United States.

NYC
WELCOME
NYC TAXI

Q
What kind of dog should direct traffic?
A
A pointer.

Now that was funny!

JOKEFINDER

Playful pups

Question-and-answer jokes

ILLUSTRATIONCREDITS

Credit Abbreviations:
DRMS: Dreamstime
GI: Getty Images
NWCM: Newscom
SS: Shutterstock

Cover: Christian Bunyip Alexander/iStockphoto/GI; back cover: (right), Catherine Ledner Photography Inc/Digital Vision/GI; (left), Panther Media Gmb/Alamy Stock Photo; spine, Wasitt Hemwarapornchai/SS

2, Csanad Kiss/SS; 4, Vauvau/DRMS; 6, (top, left), Eric Isselee/SS; 6, (top, left), Focus Stocker/SS; 6, (bottom, left), JH Lee/SS; 6, (bottom, middle), Foto Touch/SS; 7, Ots Photo/SS; 8, Jagodka/SS; 9, (top, middle), Only Food/SS; 9, (bottom, middle), Pitaksunti/SS; 10, (top, left), Helena Queen/SS; 10, (top, right), Cyno Club/SS; 10, (bottom, left), Cosmin Manci/SS; 10, (bottom, right), CK Foto/SS; 11, Zuzana Gabrielova/SS; 12, Hilary Sloan/Barcroft Images/GI; 13, (top, right), Ben Effinger/Barcroft Images/GI; 13, (middle, right), Hilary Sloan/Barcroft Images/GI; 13, (bottom, right), Hilary Sloan/Barcroft Images/GI; 14, Clearview Stock/SS; 16, (top, middle), Singjai Stock/SS; 16, (top, middle), Chones/SS; 16, (bottom, left), Margouillat Photo/SS; 16, (bottom, left), Martin Mecnarowski/SS; 17, Thka/SS; 18, (top left), Light Field Studios/SS; 18, (top, right), Cyno Club/SS; 18, (top, right), Kelvin Wong/SS; 18, (bottom, left), Susan Schmitz/SS; 18, (bottom, right), Artsilense/SS; 19, Javier Brosch/SS; 20, Alexandr Junek Imaging/SS; 21, (top, right), A6 Photo/SS; 21, (bottom, right), Smrm 1977/SS; 22, Sir Travel A lot/SS; 24, (bottom, left), Alex Hubenov/SS; 24, (bottom, left), Mary Swift/SS; 24, (bottom, right), Kuttelvaserova Stuchelova/SS; 25, Wild Strawberry/SS; 26, (top, right), Ruaridh Connellan/Barcroft Images/GI; 27, Ruaridh Connellan/Barcroft Images/GI; 28, Vjacheslav Shishlov/SS; 29, Gameanna/SS; 30, Anurak Pongpatimet/SS; 32, (top, left), Javier Brosch/SS; 32, (top, right), Andra Erickson Photography/SS; 32, (bottom, left), Isselee/DRMS; 32, (bottom, left), Eric Isselee/SS; 32, (bottom, right), Isselee/DRMS; 33, Sanjagrujic/SS; 34, (top, left), Tatyana Gladskikh/DRMS; 34, (bottom, left), Goldution/DRMS; 35, Eric Isselee/SS; 37, (top, right), JP5/ZOB/NWCM; 38, (top, left), Ermolaev Alexander/SS; 38, (bottom, left), K and Foto/GI; 39, Kobkik/SS; 40, (middle, left), Oleksiy Botko/DRMS; 40, (middle, right), Minerva Studio/SS; 41, (bottom, left), Isselee/DRMS; 41, (bottom, left), M. Unal Ozmen/SS; 41, Nejron Photo/SS; 42, Matthew Lyon/SS; 44 (top, left), Hank Frentz/SS; 44, (bottom, left), BB 1987/SS; 44, (bottom, right), Smrm 1977/SS; 45, Dmitry Kalinovsky/DRMS; 46, Masarik/SS; 48, (top, left), Bilevich Olga/SS; 48, (top, right), Judith Dzierzawa/DRMS; 48, (middle, right), P Maxwell Photography/SS; 49, Jessi et Nono/SS; 51, (top, right), CB2/ZOB/NWCM; 52, Tonie Design/SS; 54, (top, left), Mark Haughwout/DRMS; 54, (top, left), Oleg Dudko/DRMS; 54, (top, left), Exo Pixel/SS; 54, (top, right), Annette Shaff/SS; 54, (bottom, left), ESB Professional/SS; 54, (bottom, right), Outc/SS; 55, Atiger 88/DRMS; 56, Javier Brosch/SS; 57, (middle, left), Cat'chy Images/SS; 57, (middle, left), Bestv/SS; 57, (middle, right), Bilevich Olga/SS; 58, Aprescindere/DRMS; 59, Africa Studio/SS; 60, (top, right), Susan Schmitz/SS; 60, (top, right), Scol 22/DRMS; 61, Sikorsk iFotografie/SS; 62, (top, left), Eric Isselee/SS; 62, (top, right), Seregraff/SS; 62, (top, right), Nattika/SS; 62, (bottom, left), Chinmay 2012/SS; 62, (bottom, right), Am Kanobi/SS; 63, Boryana Manzurova/SS; 64, Helioscribe/SS; 66, (top, middle), Ping 198/SS; 66, (top, right), Igor Normann/SS; 66, (bottom, middle), Burhan Bunardi/SS; 67, Levente Gyori/SS; 68, Ezzolo/SS; 70, (top, left), Ayorch/SS; 70, (top, right), Nicky Rhodes/SS; 70, (bottom, left), Nastya 22/SS; 70, (bottom, right), Jagodka/DRMS; 70, (bottom, right), Interior Design/SS; 71, Oz Flash/DRMS; 72, (top, right), Steve Russell/Toronto Star/GI; 72, (middle, right), Erik Pendzich/SS; 72, (bottom, right), Jonathan Ferrey/GI; 73, Jonathan Leibson/GI; 74, (top, middle), Yazmin Mellado/SS; 74, (top, middle), Keerati/SS; 74, (bottom, middle), Twin Design/SS; 75, Anke van Wyk/SS; 76, Angyalosi Beata/SS; 78, (top, left), Graphic Photo/GI; 78, (bottom, left), Eric Isselee/SS; 78, (bottom, left), Dmytro Zinkevych/SS; 78, (bottom, right), Patjo/SS; 78, (bottom, right), Susan Schmitz/SS; 79, Natures Momentsuk/SS; 80, (bottom, middle), Aneta Pics/SS; 81, Image Db/SS; 82, Oleh Tereshchenko/DRMS; 83, (top, right), Love the Wind/SS; 83, (middle), Gyva Foto/SS; 83, (middle), Antmagn/SS; 83, (middle), Petlia Roman/SS; 83, (middle, right), Kazlouski Siarhei/SS; 83, (bottom, middle), Fernando Trabanco Fotografia/GI; 84, Mean Machine77/SS; 84, Billion Photos/SS; 84, (top, right), Gjermund/SS; 84, (top, right), Harmpeti/SS; 84, (top, right), Dutch Scenery/SS; 86, Miras Wonderland/DRMS; 87, (top, middle), Max Blender 3D/SS; 87, (top, right), Sas Partout/SS; 87, (bottom, middle), Dalius Baranauskas/DRMS; 88, (top, left), Anvar Ianbaev/SS; 88, (top, left), Ots Photo/SS; 88, (top, right), Erik Lam/SS; 88, (top, right), Hekla/SS; 88, (bottom, left), Fend Yu/SS; 88, (bottom, left), Art Nick/SS; 88, (bottom, right), Jagodka/SS; 88, (bottom, right), T Kimura/GI; 89, Eric Isselee/SS; 90, Sanjagrujic/SS; 91, (bottom, left), Pixel Robot/DRMS; 91, (middle, left), A Dogs Life Photo/DRMS; 91, (middle, right), K Tree/DRMS; 92, Chaoss/SS; 94, Zuma Press. Inc./AL; 95, (top, right), Carlos Cardetas/AL; 95, (top, middle), Carlos Cardetas/AL; 96, (top, right), Jagodka/SS; 96, (bottom, left), Henri Faure/DRMS; 96, (bottom, left), Sh El Photo/SS; 97, Zarin Andrey/DRMS; 98, Angyalosi Beata/SS; 100, (bottom, left), Maksym Bondarchuk/DRMS; 100, (bottom, left), Zurijeta/

SS; 101, Ezzolo/SS; 102, (top, left), Master1305/SS; 102, (top, right), Roland Ijdema/SS; 102, (bottom, left), Ann Anro/SS; 102, (bottom, right), Picture Pets/SS; 102, (bottom, right), Global P/GI; 103, Henner Damke/SS; 104, Annette Shaff/SS; 106, (top, left), Annette Shaff/SS; 106, (bottom, left), Grigorita Ko/SS; 107, Csanad Kiss/SS; 108, (middle, left), A Dogs Life Photo/DRMS; 108, (middle, right), Lucie Lang/DRMS; 108, (middle, right), Isselee/DRMS; 109, Ots Photo/SS; 110, (bottom, left), Ermolaev Alexander/SS; 110, (bottom, right), Sylvia Biskupek/SS; 111, Javier Brosch/SS; 112, Willyam Bradberry/SS; 114, (top, middle), Javier Brosch/SS; 114, (bottom, left), Roland Ijdema/SS; 115, Juris Didrihsons/DRMS; 116, (top, right), Paul Brown/SS; 116, (middle, right), Broad Image/SS; 116, (bottom, right), Bryan Bedder/GI; 117, John Shearer/GI; 118, (top, left), Monkey Business Images/DRMS; 118, (bottom, left), Willee Cole Photography/SS; 118, (bottom, right), Ermolaev Alexander/SS; 119, Michael Heim/SS; 120, Kamil Petran/SS; 122, (top, left), Eric Isselee/SS; 122, (top, left), Margouillat Photo/SS; 122, (top, right), BK 666/SS; 122, (top, right), Cael Paralisan/SS; 122, (bottom, left), Ingret/SS; 122, (bottom, right), S1001/SS; 123, Chutima Chaochaiya/DRMS; 124, Tham KC/SS; 126, (top, left), Dora Zett/SS; 126, (top, left), Nikolai Tsvetkov/SS; 126, (bottom, left), Bexcellent/DRMS; 127, Purple Collar Pet Photography/GI; 128, (top, right), Willee Cole Photography/SS; 128, (bottom, left), Vitaly Titov/SS; 129, (top, left), Javier Brosch/SS; 129, (bottom, right), Irina Meshcheryakova/DRMS; 130, (middle, left), A Dogs Life Photo/DRMS; 130, (middle, right), Tiffany Pettengill/DRMS; 131, Seregraff/SS; 132 (top, left), Vanessa Dualib/SS; 132, (bottom, left), Ots Photo/SS; 132, (bottom, right), Javier Brosch/SS; 133, Kawee Wateesatogkij/DRMS; 134, Wojciech Sarnowski/DRMS; 136, (top, left), Susan Schmitz/SS; 136, (top, right), Tatyana Panoca/SS; 136, (bottom, right), Isselee/DRMS; 136, (bottom, right), Johannes Kornelius/SS; 137, Eve 81/SS; 138, Amanda Edwards/GI; 139, (top, right), Astrid Stawiarz/GI; 139, (middle, right), Astrid Stawiarz/GI; 140, (top, left), Eric Isselee/SS; 140, (top, right), Sergey Fatin/SS; 140, (bottom, left), Militarist/SS; 140, (bottom, left), Nadezhda V. Kulagina/SS; 140, (bottom, right), Zoja Emelianova/SS; 140, (bottom, right), Pretoperola/DRMS; 141, Javier Brosch/SS; 142, Wild Strawberry Magic/DRMS; 144, (top, middle), Damedeeso/DRMS; 144, (bottom, middle), Red Dogs/SS; 145, Irina Meshcheryakova/DRMS; 146, Annette Shaff/SS; 147, (top, left), Masarik/SS; 147, (bottom, left), Africa Studio/SS; 147, (bottom, right), Anton Herrington/SS; 148, Aliaksei Smalenski/DRMS; 150, (top, left), Anna Mandrikyan/DRMS; 150, (top, left), Ella Batalon/DRMS; 150, (bottom, right), Oleksii Stasiuk/DRMS; 151, Pattarawat/SS; 152, A Dogs Life Photo/DRMS; 154, (top, middle), Dezy/SS; 154, (bottom, left), Metha 1819/SS; 155, Robynrg/SS; 156, (top, middle), Halimqd/SS; 156, (top, middle), Big and T/SS; 156, (bottom, left), Lakov Filimonov/DRMS; 156, (bottom, middle), Spf/SS; 157, Alan Budman/SS; 158, Stickler/SS; 160, Creativa Images/SS; 160, Susan Schmitz/SS; 162, (bottom, middle), Pieter Snijder/DRMS; 163, Red Dogs/DRMS; 164, Roma Koma/SS; 164, Ksenia Merenkova/SS; 166, (top, middle), Chaoss/DRMS; 166, (bottom, middle), Cebas 1/DRMS; 167, Grigorita Ko/SS; 168, Isselee/DRMS; 170, Annette Shaff/SS; 171, (top, left), Sergey Rasulov/DRMS; 171, (bottom, middle), Tugol/SS; 172, (top, left), Anna Mandrikyan/DRMS; 172, (top, right), Damedeeso/DRMS; 172, (bottom, left), Damedeeso/DRMS; 174, Irina Kozorog/SS; 176, (top, left), Kristina Sh/SS; 176, (top, right), Bridgena Barnard/SS; 176, (bottom, right), Rafael Ben Ari/DRMS; 177, Sikorski Fotografie/GI; 178, Dora Zett/SS; 178, Cool R/SS; 180, (top, left), Mary Rice/SS; 180, (bottom, middle), Ots Photo/SS; 180, (bottom, right), Pete Saloutos/SS; 181, Anna Bakulina/DRMS; 182, (top, right), Mark Large/SS; 182, (middle, right), Mark Large/SS; 183, PA Images/AL; 184, (bottom, left), J Staley 401/SS; 185, Scott Williams Images/SS; 186, Alexander Bukin/DRMS; 187, (bottom, right), Foto Jagodka/GI; 188, (top, left), Sir Travel A lot/SS; 188, (top, right), Harbachova Yuliya/SS; 188, (bottom, left), Nejron/DRMS; 188, (bottom, right), Marc Benson Photography/DRMS; 189, Ots Photo/SS; 190, Monika Wisniewska/SS; 192, (top, right), Wynian/SS; 192, (bottom, left), Sikorski Fotografie/SS; 192, (bottom, right), Jaclyn Wr/GI; 192, (bottom, right), Pavel Hlystov/SS; 193, Miras Wonderland/SS; 194, Atlas Pix/AL; 195, (top, right), Atlas Pix/AL; 195, (middle, right), Carlos Cardetas/AL; 195, (bottom, right), Atlas Pix/AL; 196, Lena Voynova/SS; 198, (top, middle), Damedeeso/DRMS; 198, (bottom, left), Ots Photo/SS; 198, (bottom, left), Yellow Cat/SS; 199, Ross Stevenson/SS; 200, Alexey Malashkevich/SS; 200, (bottom, left), Vitalii Mamchuk/SS; 202, (bottom, right), Global P/GI.

Since 1888, the National Geographic Society has funded more than 12,000 research, exploration, and preservation projects around the world. The Society receives funds from National Geographic Partners, LLC, funded in part by your purchase. A portion of the proceeds from this book supports this vital work. To learn more, visit natgeo.com/info.

For more information, visit nationalgeographic .com, call 1-877-873-6846, or write to the following address:

National Geographic Partners
1145 17th Street N.W.
Washington, D.C. 20036-4688 U.S.A.

Visit us online at nationalgeographic.com/books
For librarians and teachers: nationalgeographic .com/books/librarians-and-educators

More for kids from National Geographic: natgeokids.com

National Geographic Kids magazine inspires children to explore their world with fun yet educational articles on animals, science, nature, and more. Using fresh storytelling and amazing photography, *Nat Geo Kids* shows kids ages 6 to 14 the fascinating truth about the world—and why they should care.
kids.nationalgeographic.com/subscribe

For information about special discounts for bulk purchases, please contact National Geographic Books Special Sales: specialsales@natgeo.com

For rights or permissions inquiries, please contact National Geographic Books Subsidiary Rights: bookrights@natgeo.com

Art directed by Callie Broaddus and Sanjida Rashid
Editorial, Design, and Production by Plan B Book Packagers

Trade paperback ISBN: 978-1-4263-3691-1
Reinforced library binding ISBN: 978-1-4263-3692-8

Printed in Malaysia
19/IVM/1